A Messerschmitt Bf 109G-10 lands on the grass at Duxford, the Imperial War Museum's airfield near Cambridge, England.

Designed by Dan Patterson. Edited by Ross A. Howell, Jr. and Jamie L. Bronner.

Library of Congress Catalog
Card Number 97-73124

ISBN 1-57427-054-0

Printed in Hong Kong

Published by Howell Press, Inc., 1147 River Road, Suite 2, Charlottesville, VA 22901
Telephone 804-977-4006

First Printing

HOWELL PRESS

Previous page: At the top left of the photograph is a Luftwaffe high-altitude flight jacket with a bearskin lining; inside the jacket is a "flier's blouse" that dates from the Battle of Britain. At top right is a standard-issue life preserver resting on a back-type parachute harness and packed parachute. At bottom left is a pair of flight boots that also date from the Battle of Britain. At bottom right is a lightweight flying suit. At the center of the photo are a leather pilot's helmet and a pair of untinted goggles for night fighter operations. On top of the gloves are the badges of a fighter pilot. Above, the rings carry blue stones that identify the wearer as a veteran of the Russian Campaign. The ring with the gold trim is that of a senior officer.

Above: The Bf 109G-2, "Black Six." Captured in 1942 and restored to flying condition by RAF technicians in 1991, this is the only Luftwaffe aircraft with a combat record still flying.

The Bf 109 G-10 makes a low pass.

Preface

When you see the Messerschmitt Bf109 for the first time, what strikes you is how small it is. This legendary fighter airplane that was such a formidable opponent, seems unable to live up to its reputation. Compared to the Spitfire, the P-51 Mustang and certainly the P-47 Thunderbolt, it is tiny. As I worked on this book and learned about this famous fighter I discovered the ingenious designs that made this such a versatile tool, and that the skill of the pilot was paramount to its success. The "flying tail", and interconnected flaps are just some of the innovations.

My first encounter with this airplane was while working on the Lancaster book, in this series. The Bf109 G-10 photographed for this book, was being worked on at Duxford. A specialist from Germany was remounting the enormous Daimler-Benz engine onto the airframe. The engine had been removed and rebuilt after a number of mechanical problems that finally led to Mark Hanna having to land the fighter "dead stick", after seizing up completely just after taking off. It is almost hard to believe that a 2,000 horsepower engine could actually be fitted to such a small airplane.

One of the mechanics working on the fighter told me as I was working on this book, that after flying the airplane with the rebuilt engine, that the problems they had been having had vanished. They had been having wartime problems, and when it was torn down to be rebuilt, had found drill bits left inside the engine as well as other less than precise workmanship. The engine had been built by forced labor and was perhaps the target of some inside sabotage.

The subtle and not so subtle differences in aircraft design from World War II are what makes these books so interesting to work on. There is a definite style to the airplanes of different countries. American airplanes are big and functional with large engines, lots of firepower, and protection for the crewmen. British airplanes are curved and graceful, lots of guns but small caliber and the engines make the sweetest sound. The German airplanes have the look of function first, a Teutonic quality about them, engineered to be excellent, huge engines, large guns and not much creature comfort for the crew.

I can't wait to start on the next one.

Dan Patterson
May 20, 1997

MESSERSCHMITT Bf 109

Luftwaffe Fighter

Photographs by Dan Patterson

Text by Air Vice-Marshal Ron Dick

Howell Press

MESSERSCHMITT Bf 109

Descriptions of the Messerschmitt Bf 109 seldom include the word "pretty." In contrast to its contemporary and frequent wartime opponent, the Spitfire, the Bf 109 has never had the appeal of an aeronautical beauty queen. Willy Messerschmitt's brainchild has more usually been depicted as lethal looking, or having an air of menace. World War II test pilot Eric Brown went so far as to call it "sinister." Whatever impressions its appearance evoked, there is no doubting that the Bf 109 earned its place in history as one of the most outstanding military aircraft ever produced. In various forms, it fought in the Spanish Civil War and on every front of the European and Mediterranean theaters throughout WWII, gaining more aerial victories in the process than any other fighter. More than 33,000 were built, and the Bf 109 remained a force to be reckoned with to the end of its combat career.

The Bf 109's remarkable success was built on improbable foundations. For one thing, Erhard Milch, who rose to be Hitler's Secretary of State for Aviation, hated Willy Messerschmitt. In 1927, the aircraft manufacturing company Bayerische Flugzeugwerke (BFW) had been formed from a merger of the original BFW and Messerschmitt's own company. In the new organization, Messerschmitt looked after design and development, while the old BFW factory retained responsibility for production. In 1929, a series of heated arguments between Messerschmitt and Milch (then Lufthansa's Director of Procurement) over the cancellation of a Lufthansa contract led to BFW being driven to bankruptcy. The bitterness felt by the two men for each other after that never abated, and when BFW reformed it was deliberately limited by Secretary of State Milch to being a second source manufacturer of other companies' designs. In desperation, Messerschmitt solicited orders from outside Germany, and was denounced by Milch for acting counter to German interests when he negotiated Rumanian contracts. However, Germany was in the process of establishing itself as a world power in the air and could not afford to lose either the BFW factory or its chief designer. A sympathetic word from Hermann Göring helped BFW to survive.

In 1934, BFW produced the excellent Bf 108 Taifun light plane, an advanced technology monoplane design, featuring a single spar wing fitted with slotted flaps and ailerons as well as leading edge slats. The lessons learned from the Bf 108 proved crucial to the company's later success.

Bf 109 prototype. (Jeffrey Ethell Collection)

It was also in 1934 that the German Air Ministry issued specifications for a new fighter design to the Heinkel, Focke-Wulf, and Arado companies. At first, BFW was ignored, but the opinions of air force officers familiar with the Bf 108, together with Göring's helpful influence, eventually resulted in Messerschmitt being given a development contract for a fighter aircraft. Milch made it clear that a production order was unlikely to follow. Faced with such intransigence, Messerschmitt accepted the challenge of producing an aircraft which would be so superior to its competitors that it would be accepted for the Luftwaffe despite Milch's antagonism.

Messerschmitt's conception for the Bf 109 incorporated the most successful elements of the Bf 108, while wrapping the lightest and smallest airframe possible around the most powerful engine available. For the prototype this meant using the 695 hp Rolls-Royce Kestrel, since suitable engines from Junkers and Daimler-Benz were still at the development stage. (Rolls-Royce engineers, already involved with the Hawker and Supermarine companies in Britain, thereby found themselves supporting work being done on aircraft destined to become fierce adversaries just a few years later.) Flight tests of the first Bf 109A (V1) began at Augsburg in May 1935 in the hands of the factory test pilot, "Bubi" Knötsch. After their satisfactory completion, V1 ("V" for "*Versuch*s"—a designation indicating an experimental or pre-production aircraft) was flown to the Luftwaffe test center at Rechlin, where it was

initially regarded with considerable suspicion by air force test pilots.

If the Bf 109A gave a poor first impression, it was perhaps hardly surprising. Fighter pilots trained in the early 1930s had a strong bias towards the open cockpits, low wing loadings, and forgiving characters of the agile biplanes with which they were familiar. To them, the Bf 109A's confining canopy and small wing area seemed to suggest an unnecessarily demanding nature. They could see that the exaggerated angle of the fuselage when the aircraft was on the ground would make it impossible to see ahead around the relatively huge engine, and the track of the spindly undercarriage looked frighteningly narrow. They were encouraged in their fears when the Bf 109A collapsed a main undercarriage leg during landing at Rechlin. Fortunately for Messerschmitt, the damage proved to be easily repairable, and the aircraft was not grounded for long.

In the Rechlin trials, the Arado and Focke-Wulf entrants were quickly eliminated because of poor performance, and the Heinkel 112 became the front-runner. Heinkel's contender had an open cockpit, and although it was a monoplane, its wing was generous compared to the Bf 109's. It also sat on the ground at a more reasonable angle, and its undercarriage had a reassuringly wide stance. Messerschmitt's fighter silenced some of its critics when it was shown to be nearly 20 mph faster than the Heinkel in level flight, and noticeably superior in both the dive and the climb. Nevertheless, by the end of the preliminary trials, the He 112 was still favored by many to become the Luftwaffe's first monoplane fighter. As the celebrated Luftwaffe fighter leader, Adolf Galland, has pointed out: "[The pilots] could not or simply would not see that for modern [late 1930s] fighter aircraft the tight turn as a form of aerial combat represented the exception, and further, that it was quite possible to see, shoot and fight from a closed cockpit."

Unruffled by the knowledge that they were the underdogs, Messerschmitt and his staff pressed ahead with the construction of the second and third Bf 109 prototypes (V2 and V3), both powered by the Junkers Jumo 210A engine of 610 hp. The inverted "V" mounting of the Jumo eliminated the cowling bulges so evident in V1, the new streamlined shape being broken only by grooves within which, in V3, could be seen the muzzles of two rifle-caliber machine guns. The performance of all three early prototypes was almost identical—maximum speed 292 mph at 13,000 ft; service ceiling approaching 27,000 ft. As the evaluations of the rival fighters continued during 1936 at Rechlin and Travemünde, the consistently superior performance of the Bf 109 began to influence the opinions of even the most loyal Heinkel supporters. The matter was settled decisively after a final fly-off at Travemünde in the autumn of 1936. The Messerschmitt test pilot, Hermann Wurster, gave an impressively confident exhibition, including tight turns within the airfield boundary, flick rolls and tail slides at low altitude, extended spins in both directions, and terminal velocity dives with high-G recoveries. The He 112 could not match the performance of the Bf 109A in any respect and the Reichsluftministerium (RLM) board recommended the selection of Messerschmitt's aircraft for the Luftwaffe. An order followed for BFW to supply ten pre-production aircraft. The rank outsider had overcome its severe handicapping and come from behind to win.

Bf 109B ("Bertha")

The pre-production series aircraft were given the designation Bf 109B-0, and they continued the "V" codes sequence, the first of them therefore becoming Bf 109 B-01, V4. This aircraft was very similar to its immediate predecessor, a hole in the spinner revealing the presence of an additional gun mounted to fire through the propeller hub, a feature which would be retained for most of the production variants of the Bf 109 throughout its life.

For the most part, all ten of the Bf 109B-0s were used for general development work, while several served as prototypes for specific production models. They evaluated the myriad modifications which new aircraft must normally endure, and they were fitted with both progressively more powerful engines and with more efficient propellers than the original fixed pitch wooden airscrew. Later aircraft, from V10 onwards, flew with Daimler Benz DB600 series engines giving 960 hp for takeoff and were hauled along by a three-bladed variable pitch metal propeller acquired from the U.S. company, VDM-Hamilton. In this configuration, they began to reveal the true capabilities of the airframe, reaching level flight speeds of over 360 mph and service ceilings of more than 30,000 ft.

Spain

The normal Bf 109 development program made good progress during 1936, but an opportunity arose at the year's end to evaluate the new fighter in more challenging circumstances. Soon after the outbreak of the Spanish Civil War, Adolf Hitler committed his air force to the support of General Francisco Franco's Nationalist cause. Luftwaffe units (operating in Spain under the name "Condor Legion" from late 1936) faced Republican squadrons flying Soviet aircraft, and, to their dismay, the German pilots found themselves consistently outflown. Their Heinkel 51s were no match for the Polikarpov I-15s and 16s of their opponents. As a first step towards redressing

the balance, Bf 109s V3, V4, and V5 were sent to Spain for evaluation under operational conditions.

The pilot chosen to begin the evaluation was Lt. Hannes Trautloft, later a celebrated WWII fighter leader. In December 1936, the aircraft were delivered to Seville, and Trautloft wrote: "The new Bf 109 looks simply fabulous. Beside it, the good old He 51 is like a withered maiden...." However, just before Christmas, he had to admit that there were problems associated with breaking in the new fighter: "I have been in Seville for almost two weeks now, as the Bf 109 goes down with one teething trouble after another.... First the tail-wheel does not work, then the water pump, then the carburetor, then the undercarriage locking mechanism." Nevertheless, when he did manage to get airborne, his comments were full of enthusiasm for Messerschmitt's creation. "Its flight characteristics are fantastic," he said, adding on another occasion: "To fly the 109 is really a joy." Finally, on January 14, 1937, all the problems seemed to have been overcome and Trautloft flew V4 to the Madrid sector for operational trials.

By February, the prototypes were on their way back to Germany. A number of combat sorties had been flown without conspicuous success, but valuable experience had been gained in the field which eased the entry of the production aircraft into operational service. The first Bf 109 B-1s emerged from the Augsburg factory in February 1937 and were delivered to II Gruppe of the

Bf 109B carried only two machine guns, firing through the propeller.
(Jeffrey Ethell Collection)

elite "Richthofen" Jagdgeschwader, JG132. At the same time, the pleas for help from Generalmajor Hugo Sperrle, the Condor Legion commander, became increasingly insistent and it was decided to send Bf 109s to Spain as soon as practicable. After a brief period of familiarization with the new type, therefore, II/JG132's personnel found themselves on their way to Seville, where they joined 2 Staffel of Jagdgruppe 88, under the command of Günther "Franzl" Lützow. (Adolf Galland said of Lützow that he was "...the outstanding leader in the Luftwaffe." Lützow claimed five aerial victories in Spain, and achieved a total of 108 before his death in a Messerschmitt 262 in April 1945.)

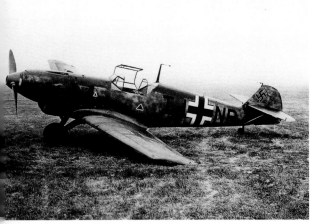

This Bf 109C fell victim to the narrow undercarriage, which caused numerous accidents. (Jeffrey Ethell Collection)

The aircraft for 2./J88 were shipped to Spain and reassembled in March 1937. Initially, the pilots regarded their new mounts with somewhat nervous enthusiasm. The Bf 109 B-1 had little in common with their unsophisticated He 51s. It had a pronounced tendency to swing on takeoff and to drop the port wing sharply if dragged roughly into the air. Indeed, it was inclined to be intolerant of insensitive handling at any time. Coarse use of the controls at speed was quickly rewarded by violent aileron shudder or by a sudden stall in a high-G maneuver. Even the experienced Lützow could be caught out. In one report he said: "I attacked out of the sun and pulled up, but too fiercely. The plane wallowed for a bit and lost speed." The first American to fly the Bf 109 was Al Williams, the Schneider Trophy racer, who in 1938 noted the need for a delicate hand: "...the touch of a pianist would be in keeping with the fineness of response," he said.

"I am sure that any ham-handed pilot who handled the controls in brutal fashion would soon be made to feel ashamed of himself." In Spain, familiarity with the Bf 109's idiosyncrasies steadily bred confidence and the pilots soon became convinced that they were flying a fighter which was vastly superior to all of its likely adversaries. That conviction was enhanced once the Bf 109 B-2 began appearing in the summer of 1937, fitted with the variable pitch metal airscrew instead of the inefficient fixed wooden propeller of the B-1.

It was not until July 1937, when countering the Republican offensive at Brunete, west of Madrid, that the Bf 109s saw serious action. During that operation and from then on, the Bf 109 units were heavily engaged in their primary duty of maintaining air superiority, but increasingly also as bomber escorts and in ground attack missions and offensive sweeps. Lützow left a graphic account of the air superiority struggle: "...mostly it was Ratas and Curtisses against my small formation. Seven against 40! There was no time to aim carefully. It was turn, attack, aim at the red circle, press the buttons, pull out, gain some height, turn back, get the next one in front of one's guns—hold it; this time too many are behind me—dive down and break away for a moment to get one's breath back." (At the time, many believed that the Soviet aircraft in Spain were actually of U.S. design. Hence, the Nationalist side often referred to the I-15 "Chato" [Snub-nose] as a Curtiss, and to the I-16 "Mosca" [Fly] or "Rata" [Rat] as a Boeing.) The Brunete battle was significant in the history of air power because it was there that fast monoplanes first clashed in earnest, with Bf 109s tackling the Republican I-16s. Below 10,000 ft, the I-16 could not match the Messerschmitt's diving abilities, but it was more maneuverable, had a better rate of climb, and was as fast as the Bf 109 in level flight. Above that height, the advantage swung to the Bf 109, as the power of the I-16's M-25 engine (a license-built Wright Cyclone R-1820) fell away. The German pilots soon found it to their advantage to use their aircraft's superior performance at altitude in claiming the "high ground," so dictating the terms of any engagement and avoiding turning dogfights by diving down on their enemies in slashing high-speed "hit and run" attacks.

More fundamentally, the higher speeds of the opposing fighters enlarged the scale of the action, so that air battles often covered hundreds of square miles instead of being the concentrated

affairs resembling swarms of gnats seen in WWI. This in turn led the Luftwaffe to devise new tactics. (In fact, they rediscovered a system first devised by Oswald Boelcke in WWI. He led open formations which fought as a team, the relatively small distances between aircraft determined by the turning radius of his Albatros.) The close "vic" formation of three aircraft (*kette*) was found to be impractical for the new fighters, and the basic fighting unit became the much looser *rotte*, a pair of aircraft comprising a leader and a wingman flying perhaps 200 yards apart. Two *rotte* made up a *schwarm* (commonly known now as "finger four"), and a *staffel* in the air was usually made up of three *schwarm*. The development of these tactical arrangements in the closing months of the war in Spain was led by Werner Mölders, who took over 3./J88 from Adolf Galland as it converted to Bf 109s in the summer of 1938. His efforts and his later reports on the success of the tactics, highlighting improvements in flexibility and in mutual support, established the system in the Luftwaffe. In so doing, Mölders set a pattern for fighter combat which was eventually adopted as standard operational procedure by every air force worldwide.

Propaganda

Political considerations prevented the success of the Bf 109 in Spain from being used for propaganda purposes, and so alternatives were pursued. In July 1937, five of the V series 109s (three Jumo-powered—V7, 8, and 9—and two with the Daimler Benz DB600A—V13 and 14) were sent to represent Germany at the 4th International Flying Meeting near Zurich. Apart from the engine failure and crash suffered by Ernst Udet in V14, the meeting was a Messerschmitt triumph. Wins were posted in the single and team "Circuit of the Alps" races, and Carl Francke won the climb and dive competition in V13, climbing to 3,000 meters (9,840 ft) and then diving to 300 meters (984 ft) in only 2 mins 5.7 secs. In a move calculated to spread international apprehension, the Germans encouraged the assumption that these world-beaters were already in general service with the Luftwaffe. In November 1937, added emphasis was given to the Zurich achievements when V13, highly polished and re-engined with a boosted DB601, set a new landplane world speed record of 379.38 mph. (Taking account of the 1937 achievements, the directors of BFW agreed in 1938 to rename the company Messerschmitt

AG, with Willy Messerschmitt as Chairman and Managing Director.) A little more than a year later, the world was astonished to hear that another variant, the Me 109R, had raised the record to 469.22 mph. This was a remarkable feat, but it was also propaganda, inviting the belief that the record had been set by a version of the Luftwaffe's standard fighter. The Me 109R was not a Bf 109 development. It was a specially prepared Me 209, a completely different aircraft described by its pilot, Fritz Wendel, as "a monstrosity" and "a vicious little brute."

"Clara" and "Dora"

After Zurich, development work concentrated on the production Bf 109 variants intended to succeed the "Berthas." Bf 109Cs and Ds were produced in a number of different forms beginning in the spring of 1938. Both were Jumo powered, the principal distinction being that the "Claras" had fuel injection systems, while the "Doras" reverted to carburetors. Armament was fitted to both models in a variety of arrangements, but wing guns were now always present as well as those mounted in the nose, some aircraft being modified to carry 20 mm cannon either in the wing positions or firing through the propeller boss. In effect, the Cs and Ds were interim models, built while awaiting a reliable supply of the more powerful DB601 engines. Small numbers were exported to Switzerland and Hungary, and forty (five Cs and thirty-five Ds) reached the Condor Legion, following in the wake of the forty-five Bs already delivered to Spain.

In the latter stages of the Spanish Civil War the opposition faced by the Luftwaffe units stiffened for a while as later model I-16s made their appearance, more heavily armed and fitted with high-altitude versions of the Wright Cyclone engines. Although Bf 109 losses increased, the essential preeminence of Messerschmitt's fighter was never seriously challenged, and the Nationalists enjoyed overwhelming air superiority as the war drew to its close. Several Luftwaffe pilots continued to establish considerable reputations, on which they would build during WWII. By the end of the war in Spain, the top German scorer was Werner Mölders with fourteen aerial victories. Among other leading pilots, Walter Ösau had eight, Günther Lützow five, and Wilhelm Balthasar seven, including four shot down in six minutes during one particularly fierce battle on February 7, 1938. Between them, the men of J88 had

accumulated a total of 314 confirmed victories and had been blooded in the art of using fast monoplanes in aerial combat.

"Emil" Emerges

In the years following the first flight of the Bf 109A, a great deal was learned about manufacturing as well as operating Willy Messerschmitt's brainchild. While combat tactics were being developed which made the most of the aircraft's strengths, the breed's design was being steadily improved in the light of front-line experience. After some delays induced by developmental problems with the Daimler Benz 601 engine, Bf 109Es began appearing early in 1939. At last it

Bf 109D-1 bearing the markings of the "Condor Legion" in Spain. (Jeffrey Ethell Collection)

was felt that Messerschmitt's fighter had reached a definitive form, and the "Emil" became the first Bf 109 version to be ordered into large-scale production. With aircraft factories at Leipzig, Kassel, Regensburg, and Wiener-Neustadt involved, production rates rose rapidly and more than 1,500 Bf 109s were manufactured during 1939.

Now that the problems with the DB601 engine had been largely overcome, the performance of the Bf 109 was much improved, and in 1939 it could be justifiably claimed that it was the world's best all-round fighter aircraft. The Bf 109E-1 had a maximum level speed of 354 mph at 16,000 ft and it could reach 20,000 ft only six and a half minutes after takeoff. Inevitable weight growth had degraded the high-speed handling qualities a little and made the turning circle radius larger, but these were small costs to pay for an

engine which delivered 1,175 hp for takeoff and was still giving almost 1,000 hp at 12,000 ft. The DB601 also had a fuel injection system, allowing negative-G flight without loss of power, an attribute for which many Luftwaffe pilots, fighting for their lives in fierce battles over Britain in 1940, would give heartfelt thanks.

Some Bf 109Es were sent to Spain, but they were too late to make any significant impact on the conflict there. The Spanish Civil War ended in March 1939, and twenty "Emils," together with twenty-seven earlier models, were handed over to the Spanish Air Force when the Condor Legion went home. Throughout that summer, the Jagdgruppen in Germany were re-equipped with the Bf 109E at a frantic pace, and when German forces crossed the Polish frontier on September 1, 1939, there were 1,056 of the new fighters in the Luftwaffe's front line. Uncertainty over the reaction of France and Britain, however, led to most Bf 109 units being held back in Germany, and it was not until Hitler launched his assault in the west on May 10, 1940, that the full strength of the Luftwaffe's fighter force was committed to battle. Before that happened, the Allies had been given a golden opportunity to find out all about the Bf 109E.

During the "Phony War" (or "Sitzkrieg," as the Germans called it) of late 1939/ early 1940, two Luftwaffe pilots separately made the mistake of landing Bf 109Es in France. Subsequent test flying confirmed that, although it could be outmaneuvered by the Hurricane and Spitfire

Bf 109E-1, shot down over England during the Battle of Britain, 1940. (Jeffrey Ethell Collection)

at low speed and low-level, the Messerschmitt was superior in most respects to all Allied fighters except the Spitfire 1 fitted with the three-bladed variable pitch propeller. Thus equipped, the Spitfire was marginally faster, and clearly the better aircraft above 20,000 ft. Even so, the Bf 109E was the steadier gun platform and delivered a far heavier punch, particularly when armed with two 20 mm cannon in the wings, as it was from the E-3 variant on. (At this stage, problems of overheating, jamming, and excessive vibration of the engine-mounted cannon could not be cured and it was not fitted.) The general opinion of the Allied test pilots who flew the Bf 109 was that it was an impressive fighting machine, although the cockpit was not admired. Eric Brown said: "The cockpit was small and narrow, and was enclosed by a cumbersome hood that was difficult to open....space was so confined that movement of the head was difficult even for a pilot of my limited stature."

As German forces swept through Holland and Belgium and conducted the lightning campaign which overwhelmed France, the Luftwaffe's Bf 109s rapidly established and continued to hold complete superiority over the Allied air forces. Even so, the intensity of operations was such that the cost was high. In May and June 1940, the Luftwaffe lost more than 1,400 aircraft, 257 of which were Bf 109s. For the first time, the Jagdgruppen had begun to meet well-trained opponents flying modern fighters and the battle had not always been one-sided. Of more than a little concern to Bf 109 pilots was the revealed vulnerability of their fighter because it lacked armored

protection, and during the summer Bf 109E-3s began to be fitted with seat armor and armor plate attached to the canopy, above the level of the pilot's head.

Battle of Britain

When France fell, it seemed only a matter of time before Britain also succumbed. While Winston Churchill broadcast British defiance, German forces gathered on the Channel coast of France. In early July 1940, after a few weeks of rest and recuperation, during which the Luftwaffe replaced its losses and redeployed to forward bases in France, the curtain rose on the first act of the Battle of Britain. It raged on until October as the Luftwaffe strove to destroy RAF Fighter Command and gain the air superiority which was a prerequisite for a successful invasion of England. It was the first (and arguably the only) strategic battle fought entirely between opposing air forces. Its outcome depended to a significant degree on the capabilities and limitations of the Luftwaffe's Bf 109 force.

Among the more obvious limitations was the short range of the Bf 109. Even operating from airfields as far forward as the Calais area, the fighters could not reach out further than London. This fact was to bedevil the Luftwaffe throughout the struggle. It soon became apparent that daylight bombing operations were only feasible within the Bf 109's radius of action, and that meant that ninety percent of Britain could not be attacked except at night, and during the hours of darkness it was impossible either to bring the RAF to battle in the air or to deliver accurate strikes against its

airfields. Thus, the Luftwaffe was hamstrung from the start. An attempt to solve the problem was made with the Bf 109E-7, which arrived in August 1940. This model was capable of carrying a sixty-six gallon plywood drop-tank, enough extra fuel to have had a marked effect on the battle, but the tank was not used. It was prone to massive leaks and the squadrons feared the risk of fire.

Heinz Lange was a pilot with JG54 in 1940. He had every sympathy with the bomber crews he was tasked to protect. "They always had to take the shortest and most predictable route to their targets because of the Bf 109's small radius of action," he remembers. Even when forcing the bombers to pay such a price, he says, running short of fuel was all too common an occurrence for fighter pilots. So much so that the standard response to a young wingman reporting that his low fuel warning light had come on was: "Well—cover it up!" New pilots exposed to the harsh reality of combat for the first time could not expect to receive any great sympathy from their battle-hardened colleagues. Edu Neumann of JG27 was once limping home with a large hole in his wing when he heard a young pilot calling plaintively that he was alone and did not know what to do. Neumann called: "Fly east! Fly east!" but a more cynical voice broke in to say: "Just wait. A Spitfire will be along in a minute and you will be alone no longer." Heinz Lange recalls several occasions when Bf 109s were lost in the Channel simply because they ran out of fuel. He agrees that an extra tank might have changed things, but smiling wryly at the memory of combat he adds: "Perhaps it was good that the drop-tanks came later. As it was, we did not have to stay so long over England!"

Looked at simply in terms of numbers, the Luftwaffe had every right to feel confident that the RAF would be defeated in 1940. The main assault on Britain was launched on August 13, named "Adler Tag" (Eagle Day) by Reichsmarschall Göring. On that day, RAF fighter Command had 620 Hurricanes and Spitfires serviceable to take on some 2,550 Luftwaffe aircraft, including almost 1,000 medium bombers, over 250 dive bombers, 224 Bf 110 twin-engined fighters, and 805 Bf 109s.

Initially, from the German point of view, the battle seemed to go well. The RAF fighters necessarily concentrated on the bombers as their primary targets, while the Bf 109s were given the freedom to ensure that they held local tactical advantage and could make the most of their diving and climbing abilities in slashing attacks against their opposite numbers. Experienced Bf 109 pilots, like Gerhard Schöpfel, Commander, III/JG26, made the most of it. "On 18 August," he says, "we saw a squadron of Hurricanes below us. They were climbing in a wide spiral near Canterbury, using the old-fashioned close formation of threes." Schöpfel chose to attack by himself, diving out of the sun and leaving his squadron to cover him from above. "Two Hurricanes were weaving behind," he recalls, "but they did not see me. I got very close before firing and shot both down in rapid succession. Then I attacked the rearmost Hurricane in the main formation, and it too went down. The RAF pilots still had not noticed anything, so I moved on to a fourth. This time I got too close, perhaps only twenty meters, and pieces of Hurricane damaged my aircraft, so I had to leave." Schöpfel had destroyed four Hurricanes of No. 501 Squadron in less than two minutes.

Without exception, Bf 109 pilots felt good about the fighting capabilities of their aircraft, and particularly about its firepower. "We were confident that the Bf 109 was superior to the Hurricane, and that it was at least a match for the Spitfire," says Heinz Lange. "We were better armed, with a 20 mm cannon, and there was no doubt about the superiority of our fuel injection system." Günther Rall, history's third-ranking fighter ace, adds: "The 109's guns were good, although in many of the later models most of the firepower was tightly grouped around the nose. This meant there was not much spread of shot, so shooting had to be accurate, and preferably from very close." When asked if firing the nose guns filled the 109's cockpit with smoke, Rall comments: "If you did it right, the other guy got smoke in *his* cockpit!"

As the air battle raged on, day after day, the simplicity of the Bf 109's task was made more complex by some unforeseen factors. For one thing, the much vaunted Bf 110 Zerstörers proved to be no match for the RAF's single-engined fighters and too vulnerable to be effective in their intended role of bomber escorts. Under attack, they were forced to fly in huge defensive circles, each trying to cover the tail of the one ahead. Fritz Losigkeit of JG26 once said: "The young pilots laughed at Göring and his love of the Zerstörers. We saw them circle quite often. Once I saw a great many locked into a circle because of only two

Spitfires." The ultimate lunacy came when Göring insisted that the 110 escorts always themselves be escorted over England by 109s.

Göring intervened again in response to complaints from bomber crews that they were being inadequately protected by the fighters. The RAF was getting through to the bombers and causing serious losses. In the first week after Adlertag, the JU 87 Stuka units alone lost forty-two aircraft, while another fourteen suffered damage and casualties. The medium bombers were getting almost as badly mauled. Adolf Galland remembered that: "Göring had nothing but reproaches for the fighter force and expressed his dissatisfaction in the harshest terms." The result was an order for the Bf 109s to escort the bombers *closely*. Schöpfel, Neumann, and Losigkeit have all recalled the loss of their free-ranging role with distaste. They were instructed to fly in close formation with the bombers and not to engage the enemy unless directly attacked. Suddenly the boot of tactical advantage was on the other foot. As Heinz Lange explains: "It was very difficult to fly close escort at the bombers' height. Now it was the Spitfires which came from high above, and we were handicapped by having to fly at the same speed as the bombers." Günther Rall is even more explicit: "We really wasted our fighters. We didn't have enough to begin with, and we used them in the wrong way. We were tied to the bombers, flying slowly, sometimes with flaps down, over England. We couldn't use our previous altitude advantage, nor our superiority in a dive. The Spitfire had a marvelous rate of turn, and when we were tied to the bombers and had to dogfight, that turn was very important."

By September, the Bf 109 units had tasks which were stretching their capabilities to the breaking point. They were expected to destroy the RAF's fighters, protect the Bf 110s, and fly close escort for the bombers. There were also Bf 109 units equipped with aircraft adapted to the fighter-bomber role, capable of carrying a single 250 kg bomb or a rack of four 50 kgs. The last straw came when the focus of the Luftwaffe's attacks was shifted from RAF bases to London, allowing the RAF the breathing space in which to recover its strength. At the same time, to force the way through to the capital, Göring often required each raid to have three times as many fighters as bombers. At the beginning of the battle, the Bf 109 force had looked impressively large, but it was now apparent that too much was being asked of

too little. Repeated predictions from Göring's headquarters that the RAF was on its last legs were daily proved wrong. Luftwaffe bomber pilots reported on their raids with sardonic humor. "Crossed the English coast at 5,000 meters," they would say, "and intercepted once more by the RAF's last fifty fighters." Heinz Lange adds: "We laughed at the confident messages from HQ. The losses mounted, doubts began, morale slipped, but the fighting did not slacken. Then, as the winter weather came, the battle went to sleep. It seemed that we had lost a lot of good people for very little purpose."

Looked at as a score sheet comparing the competing fighters, the results of the Battle of Britain show that the Bf 109 lived up to its reputation. The RAF lost close to 1,000 Hurricanes and Spitfires, most of them to the Bf 109's guns. Among many impressive combat performances by Bf 109 pilots during the battle, Werner Mölders, flying with JG51, became the first Luftwaffe ace to pass the fifty-victory mark. The Luftwaffe's total combat losses revealed the RAF's concern with getting to the bombers—1,733 aircraft of all types shot down, of which 235 were the ill-fated Bf 110 Zerstörers and 610 were Bf 109s. The Luftwaffe had failed to defeat the RAF, but Messerschmitt's fighter could not be blamed for that, despite its limitations. The failure had more to do with errors of judgment at Luftwaffe headquarters than with any shortcomings of the Bf 109.

Werner Mölders, whose slashing high-speed attacks maximized the effectiveness of the Bf 109.
(Jeffrey Ethell Collection)

Bf 109F from 6/JG27 in North Africa. (Jeffrey Ethell Collection)

Other Battles, Different Shapes

Disappointed against Britain in 1940, Hitler turned to other objectives in the east and south for 1941. Bf 109s were at the forefront of Hitler's thrust into the Balkans and the attack on Greece. In Yugoslavia, the Luftwaffe even found itself fighting other Messerschmitts for the first few days, since the Yugoslav Air Force was operating a few Bf 109Es. (This was not the only time the Luftwaffe clashed with opposing Bf 109s. The Swiss more than once were forced to defend their neutral airspace with their "Emils.") It was in North Africa, however, that the Luftwaffe faced

its next major challenge. In most of these theaters of action, "Emils" still led the charge, but the Bf 109F ("Friedrich," or sometimes "Franz") had begun to make its appearance.

Development of the Bf 109F was initiated early in 1940, when the Messerschmitt design team began a program of airframe modification intended to reduce drag and to allow the installation of more powerful Daimler-Benz engines. Most noticeably, the prominent underwing radiators of the "Emil" were decreased in height and recessed deeper into the wing, and a more streamlined engine cowling was fitted, giving a

smooth unbroken sweep from the windscreen to a new, much larger spinner. The diameter of the airscrew was reduced by some four inches by the use of broader blades, and the supercharger air intake jutted further out into the airstream to increase ram effect. A little later, the Bf 109's well-known square-cut wing shape disappeared, elliptical tips being added to reduce wing-loading. To the rear, the rudder area was slightly reduced, but the most obvious change was the removal of the Bf 109's distinctive tail-plane struts, a modification which was initially disastrous. Four early aircraft were lost after pilots had reported severe vibration. It was eventually found that the removal of the struts allowed high frequency vibration to occur at certain engine speeds, leading quickly to structural failure of the tail. The addition of simple reinforcing plates solved the problem.

As before, Messerschmitt's designers were ready more quickly than the Daimler-Benz engineers, and the first "Friedrich" was flown with the existing DB601A instead of the intended DB601E. Once the new engine appeared, it provided 1,350 hp for takeoff and could be induced to give 1,300 hp at 18,000 ft. So powered and newly streamlined, the Bf 109F was noticeably superior in performance to its predecessors at all altitudes, and was at least a match for the Spitfire V. In the Bf 109F-4, maximum speed was 334 mph at sea level, rising to 388 mph at 21,000 ft. Service ceiling was up to almost 40,000 ft, and a climb to 16,000 ft took only five minutes.

Surprisingly, "Friedrich" began life less heavily armed than "Emil." Adolf Galland bemoaned the fact that the armament: "...constituted an incomprehensible regression in the 109F compared to the E series [which] had two 20 mm cannon in the wings and two normal machine guns. The one cannon of the 109F was more modern, with a quicker rate of fire, a better trajectory, and was centrally mounted over the engine to fire through the airscrew hub. Nevertheless, there were conflicting opinions as to whether the new armament should be regarded as a step forwards or backwards. Mölders shared Udet's opinion that one centrally mounted cannon was better than two in the wings. I regarded one cannon as inadequate, particularly since I considered machine guns outdated for aerial combat ....Naturally, I recognized the advantages of centrally mounted weapons, but if the armament consisted of one cannon only, then I preferred two 'decentralized' cannons.... Not every pilot was as

Ground crews wait nearby a Bf 109G, Kuban Peninsula, Russia.
(Jeffrey Ethell Collection)

good a sharpshooter as Udet or Mölders."

One pilot who proved himself to be every bit as good a sharpshooter as Mölders was Hans Joachim Marseille, who established himself as one of the most outstanding fighter pilots on either side during the North African campaign. He first saw combat against the RAF in the Battle of Britain, during which he gained seven aerial victories and was shot down four times. A relaxed attitude to authority did not endear him to many of his superiors, but early in 1941 he joined JG27, commanded by Edu Neumann, who recognized talent when he saw it and was prepared to give Marseille his head. When JG27 was sent to North Africa, Marseille added to both sides of the score-sheet on his first mission, shooting down a Hurri-cane before being shot down himself. From then on, his natural ability asserted itself and his score rose steadily. By the end of 1941, when he had thirty-six victories, JG27 had re-equipped with the new "Friedrich," adapted for desert operations and designated Bf 109F-4/Trop. In this aircraft Marseille showed his true mettle. He was a master of the difficult art of deflection shooting, and he took full advantage of the Bf 109F's superior performance. In 1942, his claims for multiple victories in a day became commonplace, and on September 1, he accomplished the almost impos-sible, claiming seventeen aircraft shot down in the course of three sorties. Marseille's legendary achievements came to an end on September 30, 1942, when flying a Bf 109G for the first time. An oil cooler fire filled his cockpit with smoke and forced him to bail out. He struck the aircraft's tail and fell unconscious to his death on the desert below. The twenty-two year-old Marseille was credited with 158 victories in just 388 combat sorties, and was one of only eleven Luftwaffe men to be awarded the Knight's Cross adorned with Oak Leaves, Swords, and Diamonds. Walter Schroer, the second most successful fighter pilot in North Africa, said of Marseille: "...there was a genius, a flair about his flying which enabled him to exploit a situation, to shoot from almost any position." In Edu Neumann's judgment: "As a fighter pilot, Marseille was absolutely supreme."

For many Bf 109 pilots, "Friedrich" was the best of the bunch. Even as it was reaching the front line, however, the Luftwaffe was pressing for fighter aircraft of even greater speed and with better high-altitude capabilities. Messerschmitt's answer was the Bf 109G ("Gustav"), which was destined in its bewildering variety of forms to become the most numerous of the breed, account-ing for over seventy percent of all Bf 109 produc-tion. Inevitably, more power was required, and Daimler-Benz provided the DB605A. In the Bf 109G-6 this gave 1,475 hp at takeoff and 1,355 hp at 18,700 ft. In some aircraft, there was the added sophistication of nitrous oxide or water-methanol injection to provide extra boost when needed. The G-10 had a DB605D with water-methanol injec-tion, and could call on 2,000 hp for takeoff and 1,800 hp at 16,730 ft, if necessary. All this extra muscle, however, did not necessarily mean more speed. The "Gustav" had put on weight. A nor-mally loaded G-6 was over 1,000 lbs heavier than its ancestor "Emil," and although the brute power

Allied test pilots found the "Gustav" to have qualities like the little girl in the *Home Life of Longfellow*—"When she was good, she was very, very good; but when she was bad, she was horrid!" At high altitude, the "Gustav" was described as "...extremely maneuverable and pleasant to fly." On the other hand, control harmony was "poor," and "...at higher speeds elevator and ailerons are so heavy that the word 'harmony' is inappropriate." Above 300 mph "...the absence of a rudder trim-mer is severely felt," and, as speed increased in the dive, the heaviness of the controls grew until, when diving to low altitude at 400 mph or more, "all controls seemed to seize solid." Indeed, Allied pilots were known to take advantage of this un-

Bf 109G-6, Russia. (Jeffrey Ethell Collection)

of a clean G-10 gave it the capability of reaching 426 mph at 24,000 ft, it was seldom seen in such an uncluttered condition. Bf 109Gs generally had to tolerate being used as pack-mules. Bombs, rockets, gun-pods, cameras, fuel tanks, and the like were hung about the airframe in various arrangements to meet a proliferation of require-ments as the war went on. They combined to erode the good and exacerbate the bad in the "Gustav's" character. Admirable though the basic Bf 109 design was, it was being overtaken by events. It was impossible for the aging airframe to continue to meet every challenge, especially when it was increasingly likely to be tested by widely differing threats in the course of a single sortie. A "Gustav" shaped to take on four-engined bomb-ers, for instance, was unlikely to be at its best when confronted by air superiority fighters.

pleasant characteristic. On several occasions, chas-ing Bf 109s were lured into steep dives with hard pullouts near the ground. Those Luftwaffe pilots unwise enough to follow sometimes found that their room for maneuver had vanished. These failings were inherent in the basic and now elderly Bf 109 design, but the Luftwaffe's need for fight-ers was great and Bf 109Gs poured off the produc-tion lines. By late 1942, nearly seventy percent of the Luftwaffe's 900-strong Bf 109 force was equipped with "Gustavs."

"Barbarossa" and Beyond

When Hitler attacked the Soviet Union in June 1941, the Luftwaffe committed more than 1,900 aircraft to the assault, of which over 400 were single-engined fighters, mostly Bf 109 E/Fs. By the end of the first day's operations, some

1,800 Soviet aircraft had been destroyed, including 322 in aerial combat. The Luftwaffe lost a total of thirty-two aircraft. Besides aerial combat, the Bf 109s engaged in airfield attack, strafing and dropping loads of SD2 fragmentation bombs to wreak havoc among the masses of aircraft parked on Soviet forward airfields. In the air, victory scores rose rapidly. On June 30, 1941, Werner Mölders, Heinz Bär, and Hermann-Friedrich Joppien each shot down five aircraft to make JG51 the first Geschwader to surpass 1,000 destroyed in the air. (In the process, Mölders raised his personal WWII score to eighty-two, so becoming the first to exceed Richtofen's WWI total of eighty. On July 15, he made sure of his place in aviation history by being first to the century mark, excluding his fourteen Spanish victories. His 101st WWII victory was his last. Awarded the coveted diamonds to the Knight's Cross and promoted to General der Jagdfliegern [Fighter Pilots], he was killed in a Heinkel 111 crash on November 22, 1941, while en route to Berlin.) In the weeks which followed, JG53, JG54, and JG3 also reached their millennia in turn, Hannes Trautloft's JG54 "Grünherz" racing to the total with 623 Soviet aircraft shot down in the last ten days of July.

It was on Germany's eastern front that the Luftwaffe's great fighter aces—the "experten"—piled up the bulk of their huge scores. In the early months, the business of destroying the Red Air Force seemed all too easy. The Soviets were caught in a poor state of readiness, and their Air Force was a match for the Luftwaffe in neither training nor equipment. The Jagdgeschwader were confidently led by seasoned combat veterans, and they knew that their Bf 109s outclassed anything they were likely to meet. As time went on, the Red Air Force learned its trade in the hard school of bitter experience and was re-equipped with modern aircraft like the Yak-9 and La-7. In the hands of pilots like Ivan Kozhedub and Alexander Pokryshkin, these fighters were more than capable of holding their own against their German opponents. At the same time, Soviet aircraft production rates rose to prodigious proportions and the Luftwaffe increasingly began to find itself outnumbered as well as occasionally outflown. The Jagdgeschwader's task was no longer easy, but those "experten" who survived the relentless Soviet onslaught continued to score heavily, principally because they were hardly ever withdrawn from the front line, and there was never any fear of there being a shortage of targets for them to

Günther Rall, with JG52 squadron insignia visible on Bf 109. (Günther Rall Collection)

engage. The huge victory scores of the "experten" were an indication of the scale and intensity of the conflict, rather than of continuing Luftwaffe superiority.

It is no surprise that Erich "Bubi" Hartmann, the world's most successful fighter pilot, fought his battles on the eastern front. In a little over thirty months between October 1942 and May 1945, Hartmann flew the astonishing total of 1,405 combat sorties, on 825 of which he engaged the enemy. He scored 352 aerial victories, the great majority of them while flying Bf 109Gs against Soviet fighters. In the process, he survived twelve crash-landings and one bailout, mostly the result of ground fire or of hitting the debris of his victims. Since the "Gustav" was not the most agile of the Bf 109s and eastern front combat was not flown at the high altitudes where it could excel, Hartmann's record is all the more remarkable. Nor did he get off to a flying start. After one hundred sorties, he had recorded only seven kills. He did, however, take the trouble during his apprenticeship as a wingman to watch and learn from such distinguished leaders as "Paule" Rossman (ninety-three victories) and Walter Krupinski (197 victories), and to develop his own combat system. His rigid adherence to carefully thought-out principles, together with his exceptionally keen eyesight and his natural abilities as a marksman, gradually made him into a pilot who got the best out of the "Gustav," and a man the Red Air Force came to regard as a notorious assassin. As far as

Hartmann was concerned, dogfighting with the opposition was "...a waste of time." He once said: "I was hired to shoot down enemy aircraft, not to play with them." For him, the essence of fighter combat lay in seeing the enemy before being seen and then taking the time to arrange the tactical situation favorably before committing to an attack. The attacker should avoid being seen, if possible, and the attack pressed home to very short range before delivering one devastating burst of fire. Excess speed built up during the attack should be used to fly through and escape to a safe position from which to assess the situation further and decide whether further attacks would be sensible. Fighting in this way, Erich Hartmann personally destroyed the equivalent of perhaps fifteen enemy squadrons or more, and, of that enormous total, he said, "Probably as many as ninety percent of my victims never even saw me."

Erich Hartmann's unit, JG52, was an incredible fighting machine and the Bf 109G served as its primary instrument. By the end of WWII, JG52 had been credited with destroying more than 10,000 enemy aircraft, and, besides the incomparable Hartmann, its roster had included Barkhorn (301 victories), Rall (275), Batz (237), Graf (212), Lipfert (203), Krupinski (197), Schmidt (173), Sturm (157), Düttman (150), Wolfrum (137), and Dieter Hrabak (125).

Drop-tanks added much-needed range to this Bf 109G-6, over the Balkans. (Jeffrey Ethell Collection)

Assault from the West

In the battles on the eastern front, the Luftwaffe was engaged with an air force opponent almost wholly concerned with the tactical support of Soviet ground forces. In the west, it was a different kind of war. The Allied air assault on the homeland of the Third Reich was a strategic campaign largely conducted by the four-engined bombers of the USAAF by day and the RAF by night. The challenges faced by the Luftwaffe's fighters on the two fronts could hardly have been more different. The air superiority struggle waged over the contending armies in the east bore little resemblance to the problems of defending the Reich, and the demands of tackling large bombers by day and night were equally diverse. Inevitably, Bf 109s in various forms were at the forefront of the Luftwaffe's efforts to counter the ever-increasing threats menacing Germany from every side.

In 1943, as the weight of the RAF's night attacks grew and the use of "Window" (small strips of metal foil) neutralized the Himmelbett zone radars of the Kammhuber defensive line, the Bf 109 found itself pressed into the unexpected role of night fighter. Since the established night defenses were being swamped, Major Hajo Herrmann, a celebrated bomber pilot, proposed the use of day fighters against the night bomber stream as an interim measure. Herrmann's contention was that, far from trying to maintain darkness around the targets attacked by the RAF, they should be swamped by light. To

the fires burning on the ground should be added as many searchlights as possible, and brilliant flares should be fired by antiaircraft batteries or dropped from patrolling aircraft. The idea was to turn night into day and expose the bombers so that they became "like flies crawling across a tablecloth." In such conditions, the day fighters could operate almost as normal. They merely had to be vectored towards the RAF's target for that night and left alone to rampage among the bombers like "Wilde Sau" (Wild Boars).

At one time in 1943, there were three "Wilde Sau" wings—JG 300, 301, and 302—flying single-engined fighters at night. Their operations did not last for long, but they served their purpose and led to more effective night-fighting techniques. Luftwaffe night fighters were freed from the rigid controls of the Himmelbett system and went on to develop the highly effective "Zahme Sau" (Tame Boar) hunting techniques which imposed heavy losses on RAF Bomber Command in 1943-44. One of the most serious drawbacks to "Wilde Sau," and one reason for its abandonment, was that many of the young fighter pilots found that flying the "Gustav" at night was too much for them. The G-6/N was a Bf 109 modified for night flying with exhaust dampers and flame shields, and fitted with the Ruestsaetz 6 conversion kit and a Naxos Z receiver. The R6 incorporated a pair of MG 151 20 mm cannon in underwing gondolas, and the Naxos Z, which homed on to the H2S radar transmissions of RAF bombers, added a

dome just aft of the cockpit. The extra weight of all this equipment did not improve the already mettlesome character of the G6, and an unacceptable number of aircraft were lost in catastrophic landing accidents. Many inexperienced pilots bailed out rather than attempt landing in bad weather or because they had become lost in the unfamiliar darkness.

Herrmann himself, the old bomber pilot, seemed to revel in the "Wilde Sau" experience. Comparing his Bf 109 to a thoroughbred horse, he wrote: "How easily I was being borne aloft! This, I thought as I looked ahead through the bullet-proof windscreen and along the slender neck, a bluish mane flaming out from the exhausts—this is breeding!" He was equally enthusiastic about the turning of night into day and the effects of the Bf 109's armament: "...I saw our first illuminating flare—the second—the third—and more. Splendid! I could see a heavy approaching from the south. I swept in astern of it, throttled back, dived, and fired into its wings and cockpit, a burst of several seconds. My aim was good. I pulled up over him, and a large object flew past my aircraft. 0257 hours: I reported a probable kill. I turned into the bright, color-filled arena. Just below me and between 500 and 1,000 meters away I saw another bomber silhouetted against the 'shroud' [of brightly lit cloud]. For a few seconds our flares dazzled me, then I opened up. The bomber caught fire. I gave a further burst. The bomber was blazing furiously: it was 0305 hours and I reported one bomber destroyed."

Courageous tactician though he was, Hajo Herrmann would not claim to have been among the most successful night fighter pilots. He was not a natural marksman and, in his determined night jousting with the enemy, he was hit by gunfire twice and had to bail out each time. The outstanding "Wilde Sau" pilot in the Bf 109 was Friedrich-Karl Müller, who was eventually credited with a total of 140 victories. Thirty of his kills came in the course of just 52 night sorties, and 23 of those were during Bf 109 "Wilde Sau" operations.

American Armadas

The problems posed by the B-17 and B-24 formations of the USAAF in their daylight raids were entirely different from those set by the RAF at night. Tightly packed together and bristling with .50 caliber machine guns, they were a fearsome sight for any fighter pilot. A solution was suggested by Egon Mayer as early as November 1942, before the 8th Air Force had even begun its campaign against Germany itself. He decided that the most effective way to penetrate the defensive screen of the bomber formations was to attack from head-on, where the enemy's firepower was weakest. He turned in well ahead of the bombers, picked a target on the fringes of the formation, held his fire until the last possible moment, triggered a burst of no more than two seconds, and broke away downwards, flashing by the American gunners at crossing speeds of 600 mph or so. Flying Bf 109s in JG2 together with Georg-Peter Eder, he developed the method, and, as the 8th AF offensive gathered momentum in 1943, it became the Luftwaffe's favored tactic.

In its close-support role, this Bf 109G-6, III/JG3, carries underwing rocket tubes. (Jeffrey Ethell Collection)

Mayer and Eder were eminently successful against four-engined aircraft. Before he was shot down and killed by a P-47 in March 1944, Mayer had a total of 102 victories, of which twenty-five were 8th AF bombers. Eder survived the war with a reputation for being both a giant killer and the Luftwaffe's most chivalrous officer. His seventy-eight confirmed victories included thirty-six four-engined bombers, but he paid a high price for his persistence against the B-17s and B-24s. Their gunners shot him down nine times. He was, however, a consummate survivor, living to tell the tale after being shot down seventeen times in all and wounded on fourteen occasions. Less hardened pilots were not usually so determined. Albert Grislawski, flying Bf 109Gs with JG50, describes the shock of a first engagement with B-17s: "It was my first view of an American formation. There were so many of them that we were shaken to the marrow ....We started making frontal attacks on the right-hand side formation; we went in in fours. I noticed that some of our new pilots broke off too soon and we never saw them again. They hadn't the heart for the tracer we had to fly through."

To make them more effective against the USAAF's bombers, the firepower of the Bf 109s was increased. G-6 modifications, for instance, included the G-6/R2, with two 21 cm mortars under the wings, and the G-6/R4, with two 30 mm cannon in pods. While these lethal extras did indeed make the Bf 109 a formidable weapon for bomber crews to face, they were a severe handicap once USAAF fighters appeared over Germany. Bf 109s equipped as bomber-killers had sacrificed their ability to take on P-47s and P-51s. The increased drag and weight made them relatively slow and ponderous, and easy meat for the USAAF escorts.

Against unescorted formations, the Luftwaffe's day fighters could be deadly, and never more so than during the 8th AF raids against Regensburg and Schweinfurt on August 17, 1943, when rank after rank of Bf 109s and FW 190s formed up and charged the enemy like Napoleonic cavalry. Heinz Kemethmüller, III/JG26, took part in an early assault on the B-17s of the 100th and 385th Bombardment Groups: "My Staffelkapitän selected a "Pulk" (formation) and led us round to the front of it. He decided which bomber he was going for and the rest of us spread out and selected ours. I just had time for one burst on mine and I saw pieces flying off one engine. I broke off high and to the right and circled....I looked at the bomber I had attacked on the first pass and saw black smoke pouring from the engine I had hit. It had started to lose height and was turning away from the formation. It was quite clear to me that it would never get home."

On the receiving end, John Brady, a pilot with the 100th BG, remembers: "They kept coming in, a steady stream of them at 12 o'clock level. When they got to their break-off point they dipped down and under. A couple of the hot-dogs rolled as they passed under us....It kept on for what seemed to be an eternity. That was one of those days I wished I'd been a gunner with something in my hand, instead of just sitting there, driving, going straight ahead into those fighters."

Being inside a B-17 when it was hit during a head-on attack could be terrifying: "They came at us from 12 o'clock high, out of the sun, and came barrel-rolling through the formation. There was an explosion near where I was and it knocked me over backwards. A 20 mm had come through the roof and exploded in the floor. I had several pieces of metal in me.... Through a hole, I could see flames coming back from something burning further forward. I don't remember feeling any panic. Things happened too fast." (Albert Van Pelt, gunner, 390th BG)

At the end of the day, of the 376 B-17s dispatched on the Regensburg/Schweinfurt raids, sixty had been shot down, and at least ten more had to be written off because of battle damage. Over eighty percent of the destruction was brought about by the Luftwaffe's single-engined fighters, more than half of which were Bf 109Gs. In return, the B-17 gunners destroyed perhaps twenty-one fighters, thirteen of them "Gustavs."

There were many other days in 1943 when USAAF bomber crews had to grit their teeth and run the Luftwaffe's gauntlet to reach targets deep inside Germany. Punishing losses were suffered repeatedly, forcing the thought that daylight bombing was not a feasible proposition after all. In 1944, the pendulum swung finally in the USAAF's favor with the arrival of the P-51 Mustang—an aircraft which could outfly the Luftwaffe's fighters but had the range of a strategic bomber. Now the destruction of the Luftwaffe began in earnest. German loss rates rose alarmingly. In April 1944, Adolf Galland reported: "The day fighters have lost more than 1,000 aircraft during the last four months, among the pilots our best officers, and these gaps cannot be filled. During each enemy raid we lose about fifty fighters. Things have gone so far that the danger of a collapse of our arm exists." During the five months before the D-Day invasion, no fewer than 2,262 German fighter pilots died. With losses like that, the Luftwaffe was irrevocably on the slippery slope to defeat.

As the losses increased, so did production rates. In 1944, the astonishing number of 13,942 Bf 109s was accepted from German factories. Others were produced in Hungary and Rumania. The problem was finding pilots competent to fly them in combat. Even the "experten" were finding that Bf 109s, thoroughbreds though they were, had been stretched to their developmental limits and overtaken by newer designs. In 1944, it was no longer possible to claim, as in 1939, that Messerschmitt's single-engined fighter was the best in the world. The matchless "Emil" had become the workhorse "Gustav."

Odds and Ends

Even as the "Gustav" was being modified into its many forms, other variations on the Bf 109 theme were being developed. Interesting though some of them were, they were not ordered into production. The Bf 109H was intended as a high-performance high-altitude fighter. Additional center sections added 11 ft to the wingspan, and the track of the undercarriage was almost doubled. Several examples of "Gustav" airframes modified to "H" standard were delivered for operational testing and were found to have service ceilings of more than 47,000 ft. However, the program was terminated soon after serious wing-flutter led to the loss of a wing in a high-speed dive, and the high-altitude role was left to the Focke-Wulf Ta 152H.

Earlier in the war, tests had been conducted with Bf 109s in an assortment of unusual configurations, including the fitting of skis, a tricycle undercarriage, a V-shaped "butterfly" tail, and alternative engines, such as the BMW801 radial and the Jumo 213 with an annular radiator. For the "Jabo-Rei" (extended range fighter-bomber) adaptation, ground clearance to allow the carriage of a 500 kg bomb was provided by

fitting a stalky tail wheel at the fuselage midpoint. Once airborne, the now surplus wheel was jettisoned by firing explosive bolts. (What happened if the bomb could not then be dropped is a matter for some speculation!) A still more dramatic method of adding to the fighter's firepower was the "Mistel" program, in which a Bf 109F was mounted on top of a Ju 88 bomber carrying an 8,000 lb warhead in its nose. The 109 pilot guided the whole contraption to the target area before releasing his lethal cargo in a shallow glide. Several of these weapons were used against Allied shipping, and others later attacked bridges over the Neisse and Rhine as the Allied armies advanced into Germany. The attacks on the bridges used by the Soviet Army were

A Bf 109K-4, at war's end, near Lechfeld, Germany. (Jeffrey Ethell Collection)

accompanied by ten Bf 109s flown by volunteers who deliberately flew their bombed-up aircraft into the targets, the only time that Luftwaffe pilots actually engaged in planned suicide missions.

When WWII began, it was the German intention to operate aircraft carriers. Two were to join the fleet in 1944. Messerschmitt was instructed to provide the Kriegsmarine with a carrier-borne version of the Bf 109. This was the Bf 109T "Toni," which was a modified "Emil." Extended wings and increased slot and flap areas improved low-speed handling, and there were manual wing-folding points, catapult attachments, and arrester hooks. The Fieseler company was given a production order for sixty "Tonis," but when the carrier program was abandoned the

aircraft were completed without their marine equipment. Designated T-2s, they were based in Norway and Heligoland, and Hajo Herrmann reports bailing out of one during his "Wilde Sau" operations.

The Bf 109Z "Zwilling" (Siamese Twins) was an attempt to produce a heavy long-range fighter without going through a completely new design and manufacturing process. Two Bf 109Fs were mated together and the resulting aircraft promised great things, but the completed "Zwilling" was badly damaged in an air raid before flight trials began and the project was never completed. (The concept was proved by a similar development of the P-51 Mustang in progress at

the same time. It was operated successfully as the F-82 and saw combat in the Korean War.)

End of the Line

The "Gustav" was the most numerous of the Bf 109 family, but it was not the last to enter production. In an effort to eliminate the confusing proliferation of sub-types and standardize on a basic 109 model, the Bf 109K was introduced, based on the G-10 variant. Most obvious changes were the clear-vision "Galland" canopy, an enlarged tail, and an elongated tail-wheel strut to raise the tail higher during takeoffs and landings. Packed under the cowling was a massive DB605ASCM which could offer 2,000 hp for takeoff. With the basic airframe standardized, there was neverthe-

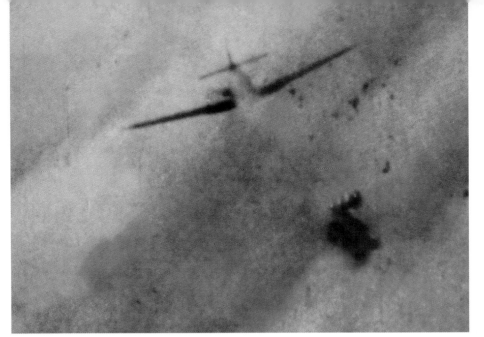

Gun camera footage of Luftwaffe pilot baling out before his Bf 109 explodes. (Jeffrey Ethell Collection)

less a need for the Bf 109K to fulfill various duties, and several sub-types appeared. The K-2 and K-4 versions were intended for use in the day fighter/fighter-bomber/long-range interceptor roles, depending on the presence or absence of bombs or drop-tanks, and differed only in that the K-4 had a pressurized cockpit. The K-6 was a more heavily armed bomber interceptor, with additional cannon in the wings to supplement the armament grouped in the nose. The K-14 was fitted with the long-awaited DB605L engine with a two-stage supercharger. In this form, the Bf 109K reached a remarkable 450 mph at over 37,000 ft.

Positive though these developments seemed, they could not put back the clock. By late 1944, when the first Ks came off the assembly line, the great days of the Bf 109 were memories. In the hands of a few remaining "experten" and young pilots hastily and inadequately prepared by the flying schools, they fought on until the last days of the war, but two operations exemplified the desperate straits reached by the Luftwaffe in 1945. Operation "Bodenplatte" was launched on January 1, 1945. It was aimed at forward Allied airfields in Belgium and Holland and was carried out by about 900 aircraft, mainly Bf 109s and FW 190s, a large percentage of which came from units trained for aerial combat and not for ground attack. Nevertheless, "Bodenplatte" caught the Allies by surprise and caused much destruction, with more than 200 Allied aircraft being destroyed or damaged on the ground. For the Luftwaffe, however, the operation was a disaster. Perhaps a third of the attacking fighter force was lost. Two hundred thirty-seven fighter pilots were killed, missing, or taken prisoner, and eighteen wounded. Among those lost were three

Geschwader, six Gruppe, and eleven Staffel commanders, men who were literally irreplaceable. The back of the Luftwaffe's fighter force was effectively broken.

As the inevitable end approached, Hajo Herrmann came forward once again with a radical proposal to form a number of "ramming groups." He intended to use up to 800 Bf 109Gs and Ks in one massive operation against the USAAF's bombers. The idea was for each fighter pilot to strike a bomber's fuselage just ahead of the tail with a Bf 109 wing. If only half the rammers succeeded in reaching their targets, some 400 bombers would be destroyed at one blow, and many of the Bf 109 pilots could count on surviving by bailing out. It would take the Americans weeks to recover from the shock of such a loss. Sonderkommando Elbe was established, initially with three Gruppen, each with forty-five pilots. The speed of advance by the Allied armies caused the force to be used too early, on April 7, 1945, when about 120 Sonderkommando Elbe Bf 109s were scrambled to attack more than 1,300 B-17s and B-24s. American records suggest that ramming destroyed eight and damaged fifteen bombers. About 100 Luftwaffe fighters were claimed destroyed during the day, and many of them were Bf 109s from the ramming unit. The operation was not mounted again.

In May 1945, almost ten years to the day since the Bf 109's first flight, the combat career of the Messerschmitt fighter came to an end. Several hundred of them sat on German airfields and in storage units. Rendered impotent by lack of fuel, they waited for Germany's collapse.

Willy Messerschmitt's design soldiered on with other nations for a few more years. Czechoslovakia manufactured Bf 109-G12s/14s with the designation CS199/S199 and operated the type until the mid-1950s. Israel bought some S199s to serve as stopgap fighters until 1949. The principal post-WWII operator, however, was Spain. Hispano Aviación manufactured the Bf 109G-2 under license but was forced to substitute a 1,300 hp Hispano-Suiza engine when DB605As were not available. The resulting HA-1109 aircraft was not a happy marriage, and in 1953 the Bf 109 came full circle when the decision was made to re-engine the fighter, re-designated HA-1112, with a 1,600 hp Rolls-Royce Merlin. So modified, the aircraft served with Spanish squadrons until 1967.

Having started life with the Rolls-Royce Kestrel and flown its first operations in Spain, it could be said that the Bf 109 had in some ways returned to its roots. There was also a touch of irony in the fact that the Luftwaffe's most numerous fighter survived powered by a version of the engine which, in aircraft like the Spitfire and Mustang, had been a major factor in its WWII defeat.

Günther Rall

Günther Rall is the fighter pilots' fighter pilot. His impressive WWII total of 275 enemy aircraft shot down places him third in the world ranking of "aces" and is more than adequate proof of his remarkable abilities as a combat pilot. However, there is more to it than that. Spare and active, even in his eightieth year, he still looks the part. Energy and enthusiasm radiate from the man, and he is keenly aware of all that happens around him. His memory is clear and sharp, and when he talks of his Luftwaffe experiences, his lively manner brings the stories to vivid life. He has many stories to tell. Taking account of both his WWII combat and his postwar career in the new Luftwaffe, it can be argued that Günther Rall is the most successful fighter pilot who ever lived.

Born in Gaggenau, Baden, on March 10, 1918, Günther Rall left school in 1936 and joined the army to become an infantry officer. Two years later he had seen the error of his ways and transferred to the Luftwaffe. As he said: "Flying seemed to have a future—as well as getting you out of the mud!" He gained his wings in 1939 and was posted to JG52. His first taste of combat came when flying the Messerschmitt Bf 109E from Mannheim with III/JG52 in the Battle of France, and on May 12, 1940, he achieved his first aerial victory. In a dogfight with a French squadron, he shot down a Curtiss P-36.

After the fall of France, his squadron moved to a base near Calais and prepared to take on the RAF. Once the Battle of Britain was joined, JG52 engaged daily in fierce combat, and soon lost its CO and two squadron commanders. With no outside replacements available, Günther Rall became the leader of his squadron at the age of twenty-two. After the Battle of Britain, JG52 was withdrawn from the Channel coast to rebuild, and later transferred to southeast Europe. They saw action in Rumania and over Crete before moving on to southern Russia and the German offensive in the Crimea. With thirty-six victories to his credit at this stage, Günther Rall's career nearly came to an end. On November 28, 1941, he says, he got careless. He followed a Soviet victim of his to see the crash and was caught by another Red Army fighter. Shot down in his turn, Rall bellied the Bf 109 onto rough ground and bounced into a small valley, smashing into the far slope. His back was broken in three places and he was told that he would never fly again.

Luftwaffe ace Günther Rall sits once again in the cockpit of a Bf 109. All of his 275 victories were achieved in this fighter type.

Determined to prove the doctors wrong, Rall was back with his unit by August 1942. One month after his return, his victory score stood at sixty-five and he was awarded the Knight's Cross. The Oak Leaves followed when he reached 100 by the end of October. In the following months, JG52 fought in the Caucasus, at Stalingrad, over the Kuban, and at Kursk, covering the German Army first in its conquests and then its defeats, and Rall's list of victories lengthened steadily. He was promoted to command III/JG52 in April 1943, and awarded the Swords for his 200th victory in September. With forty shot down in October, he raced to 250, reaching that number second only to Walter Nowotny.

Early in 1944, Günther Rall was transferred to Germany's western front and became Commander of II/JG11, flying the Bf 109G against the Allied fighters escorting the massive 8th AF formations attacking Germany. During the closing weeks of the war, he was promoted to major and given command of JG300. His final victory total of 275 was achieved in the course of some 800 operational missions, more than 600 of which involved combat. His striking rate was impressive, and compares favorably with the performance of his peers—Hartmann's 352 in 1,405 missions, and Barkhorn's 301 in 1,104. However,

Günther Rall during World War II.

Günther Rall and ground crew celebrate his 200th aerial victory.

Günther Rall relaxes between missions.

After bullets from a P-47 severed his thumb, Rall visits his mother.

On another occasion, he closed on a Russian fighter thinking it might be an FW 190 and saw the red star insignia at the last moment. He turned hard into his enemy, and: "...there was an ear-splitting, terrifying crash. I bounced on the Russian from above. I cut his wing with my propeller, and he cut my fuselage with his propeller. He got the worst of it, because my propeller went through his wing like a ripsaw. Losing his wing, he went into a spin from which he had no hope of recovery. I was able to belly in before my fuselage gave way...."

Heinz Bär (220 victories) was an outstanding contemporary of Günther Rall. In his opinion: "Günther Rall was *the* best—unsurpassed—at angle-off gunnery. He was fantastic. His wingmen were awed by his ability to shoot across a circle. He seemed to have mastered the art of measuring precisely the speed and distance of the enemy, and then to aim far enough ahead of him to have the proper lead. He would fire a few shots and *poof!*—no more enemy. Yes, Rall was the best."

Years later, when West Germany became a NATO nation, Günther Rall returned to his profession. He rejoined the new German Air Force as a major, converted to current jet aircraft and led the team which introduced the Lockheed F-104 to his service. From 1970 to 1974, in the rank of Generalleutnant, he served as Chief of the German Air Force. Few airmen have achieved so much as Günther Rall. In war and peace, he has reached the heights.

(Postscript: In 1996, during a visit to Washington, D.C., Günther Rall was invited by the USAF to try out the cockpit simulator for the F-22. Once established in the seat, he was eager for action. Given the problem of four "bogies" approaching him head-on, he acquired and dispatched them all with great speed and chilling efficiency. He smiled broadly, and suggested that he now had 279.)

he was not always the victor. He made seven forced landings and then came near disaster in a battle against 8th AF fighters near Berlin on May 12, 1944. Bullets from a P-47 shattered his cockpit and severed his left thumb. Rall bailed out, only to be threatened by a pitchfork-wielding farmer when, bleeding profusely, he reached the ground. He was out of action until the end of the year.

Günther Rall has vivid memories of other close shaves. An attack on a P-39 in Russia almost led to his incineration after his burst of fire had struck home. There was: "...a gigantic sheet of flame at least one hundred meters long, and I had no option but to rush into it...at that time the ailerons on the Bf 109 were fabric, and when I came out on the other side of that fantastic fireball there was no fabric on my ailerons, just the metal structure...the paint on my aircraft was blistered off as though a blowtorch had passed over it from nose to tail...."

Walter Schuck

Walter Schuck is not as well-known as many of his contemporaries, which is surprising in view of his WWII achievements. He flew the Bf 109 with JG5 on the more northerly reaches of the eastern front. Renowned in the Luftwaffe for his aggressive spirit and determination to engage the enemy, Schuck scored 198 confirmed victories against the Soviet Air Force. In the process, he was awarded the Knight's Cross and the Oak Leaves.

Towards the end of the war, he converted to the Me 262 jet fighter and added at least eight more victories in the west, four of them four-engined bombers. Perhaps thirty more kills were unconfirmed, largely because of Schuck's practice of conducting high-speed sweeps through the middle of the USAAF's bomber boxes, when the matter of confirmation was not always uppermost in either his mind or his wingman's.

Walter Schuck pats the side of what he calls "a good airplane." Most of his 206 confirmed victories came while flying Bf 109s, but the last eight were in the Messerschmitt 262, the world's first operational jet fighter.

Günther Rall and Walter Schuck shake hands. Between them, these two pilots accounted for nearly 500 aerial victories in World War II.

Following pages: The Bf 109G-2 "Black Six," its Daimler-Benz 605 engine warming up before taxiing. Since "Black Six" was captured in Libya, the air scoop just above the leading edge on the wing has a tropical filter to keep sand from entering the blower.

The Bf 109G-10 was a later production version with a higher vertical stabilizer, installed to give the pilot more rudder authority on takeoff and landing. Also seen is the Galland canopy, designed to improve the pilot's all-round visibility. The G-10 had a 2,000 hp engine, a remarkable amount of power for such a small airframe.

Vorsicht beim Öffnen
Kühler ist im Haubenteil eingebaut

A

B

A   The narrow track undercarriage of the Bf 109. Nearly half of all 109 losses during the fighter's operational life were due to accidents on the ground. The main wheel legs are attached to the fuselage and retract outwards. The wheel wells are lined with canvas covers which zip out for access.

B   The red markings on the main wheel legs of the G-10 give an indication of the pressure in the oleo system which cushions the landing.

C   The G-10's tail wheel leg is considerably longer than that of earlier 109s. Together with the taller fin, this helped to make the G-10 easier to control on the ground.

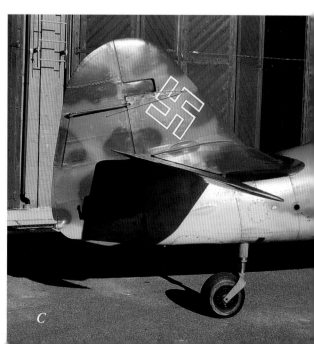

C

B

A   The vertical stabilizer of "Black Six."
No rudder trim control was fitted to the
Bf 109. The stabilizer is visibly offset
from the aircraft's center line and is
airfoil-shaped, creating sideways lift as a
counter to the considerable engine torque.

B   During preflight, the pilot always
checks the control surfaces for full and
free movement. One of the innovations
introduced by Messerschmitt in the Bf
109 was the "flying tail." Capable of
being moved several degrees up and down,
the entire horizontal stabilizer can be
trimmed from the cockpit. Bf 109 wheel
tracks are seen in the grass behind the
pilot.

C   The small rudder and stabilizers of
"Black Six."

B

A   From the F variant on, the Bf 109 was fitted with a complex and interconnected system of flaps. The smaller inner flaps were split lengthwise, the lower half being capable of moving independently to fulfill the function of a radiator flap. Note the black smudges behind the exhaust stubs. Bf 109s were notorious for being "dirty" aircraft. In combat, significant alterations of power could be detected by enemy pilots because the 109's exhaust smoke gave away throttle movements. This characteristic sometimes led to optimistic claims of 109s being shot down when they were last seen "trailing smoke." A Luftwaffe pilot's claim that the 109 could run away from a Spitfire brought the retort: "No problem. I just follow the smoke trail."

B   The leading edge slats of the Bf 109 were never under the direct control of the pilot. They deploy to smooth out the airflow over the wing whenever a high angle of attack is reached, as it is during the landing approach or in steep turns.

A

FRIEDRICH KARL MÜLLER

B

A   The cockpit and canopy of Bf 109G-2 "Black Six." Nearly all 109s were fitted with these heavy, narrow canopies, the thick bracing creating significant blind spots for the pilot and the whole limiting his head movements.

B   On the Bf 109G-10, the Galland hood offered much-improved visibility, but it was still inferior to the bubble canopy fitted to Allied fighters like the P-51D and Typhoon.

C   The armored glass of the Bf 109's windscreen is 90 mm thick.

D   A Messerschmitt mechanic once wondered whether "Willy" Messerschmitt cared much for pilots, since his design gave them very little room.

Following page: A Duxford hangar scene creates an atmosphere reminiscent of the days when Bf 109s were plentiful.

C

D

Günther Rall

37

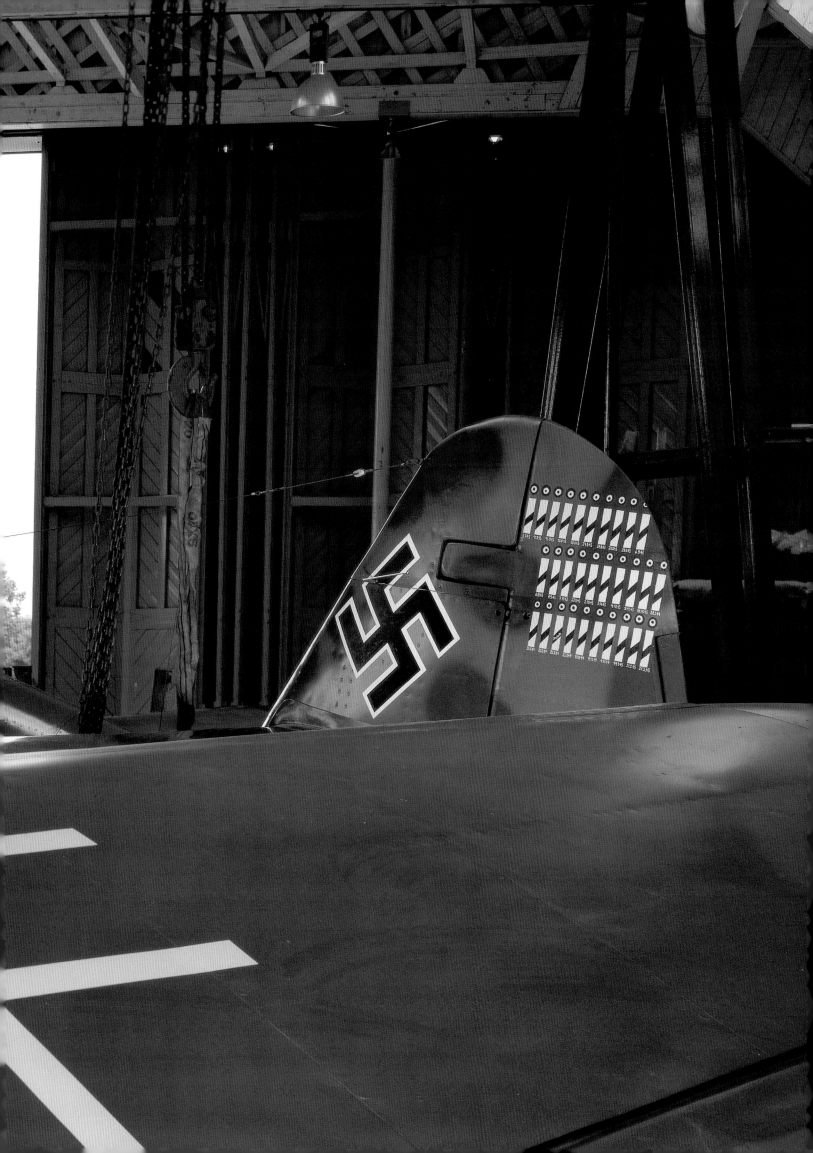

The Daimler-Benz 605D engine of the Bf 109G-10. This massive inverted-V engine, hung from a curved support just under the cowling, was capable of developing 2,000 hp at takeoff. The circular component at the back of the engine is the blower for the turbosupercharger, which pumps high-pressure air into the engine when needed, boosting available power at the high altitudes where combat often took place. The fairing visible under the open cowling is for one of the two 13 mm machine guns mounted above the engine and synchronized to fire through the propeller. The surprisingly small paddle-bladed propeller was remarkably efficient at converting engine power into usable thrust.

A   Viewed from the side, the impressive size of the Daimler-Benz 605D in relation to the airframe is readily apparent. The air scoop for the blower is visible above the open cowling. The silver container strapped to the engine is the coolant header tank. The ingenious clamshell cowling is secured tightly over the engine with just four locking clips, comparing very favorably with the seemingly endless rows of Dzus fasteners needed for the cowling of a Mustang or a Spitfire.

B   The blower for the turbosupercharger spins at extremely high rpm. Its whine gives the Daimler-Benz a distinctive sound, very different from the refined snarl of a Rolls-Royce Merlin or the rumble of a radial engine. The exhaust stubs of the inverted-V are towards the bottom of the picture. At bottom left are control linkages which run through the firewall from the cockpit.

C   A technician attends to the G-10 under an engine hoist. The Bf 109 was easy to service in the field, and an experienced ground crew could change an engine in as little as two hours.

A

B

A   The Daimler-Benz 605A engine in the Bf 109G-2 can develop 1,475 hp at takeoff. This engine, original to "Black Six," was rebuilt during the lengthy process of restoring the aircraft to flying condition. After the rated hours to the next major overhaul have been flown, it is planned for "Black Six" to be grounded and retained only as a static exhibit.

B   "Black Six," engine cowlings open, stands beyond the fin of Duxford's Bf 109G-10.

C   To start the engine of a Bf 109, a ground crewman must first crank the flywheel of the inertial starter. The removable red cranking handle seen here must be wound vigorously. When flywheel rpm reach the appropriate speed, the pilot engages the starter. If the engine is properly primed, it should start. The unit insignia at top right is that of III/JG77, which operated "Black Six" before its capture in 1942.

D   The cowling of the engine and one of the locking clips. The small intakes conduct cooling air into the engine compartment, while the spinner, much larger than those fitted to early Bf 109s, helps to streamline the airflow over the nose.

E   The manufacturer's plate is placed just aft of the engine compartment.

A

A   The Bf 109G-10's main armament, a 20 mm cannon with 150 rounds of ammunition, is mounted in the engine's inverted-V and fires through the propeller boss. (Some Bf 109Gs carried a heavier 30 mm cannon with only 60 rounds.) To the right of the upper propeller blade can be seen the muzzle of the left-hand 13 mm machine gun. Cannon shells were usually deadly to enemy aircraft. Although the muzzle velocity was not as high as that of a machine gun, the explosive shells could cause dramatic damage. It took only a few well-placed cannon shells to bring down a B-17 Flying Fortress, for example.

B   The Bf 109G's armaments were placed close to the aircraft's center line. Since the spread of shot was not great, the fighter had to be aimed accurately to hit the target. Most Messerschmitt aces got very close before firing to minimize the problem of the lower-velocity cannon's ballistics and so ensure success.

C   The 13 mm machine guns, each with 300 rounds, are placed above the engine. Here, on "Black Six," the left-hand gun is seen in its mount.

D   The breech of the cannon was placed between the rudder pedals and the pilot straddled the weapon. Here it is seen just forward of the control stick, with the left rudder pedal alongside.

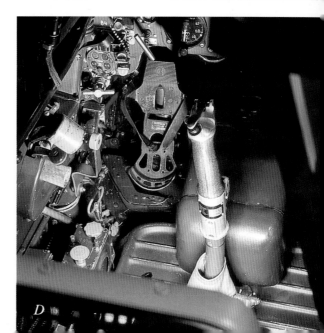

Jeffrey Ethell Collection

A

A   The cockpit of Bf 109 "Black Six" shows its snug fit for the average-size pilot. Straight ahead is the neatly arranged instrument panel. Top row—gyro compass, artificial horizon, manifold pressure gauge. Second row—altimeter, airspeed indicator, tachometer, clock, and combined coolant/oil temperature gauge. Just below are the fuel and oil gauges, and the silver handle to the left is the emergency undercarriage lowering handle. At center is the control stick, with the bomb-release button on top, and the gun-firing trigger on the front of the grip. On the floor, just ahead of the stick, is the cover for the breech of the cannon.

B   The cockpit of the Bf 109 displayed at the U.S. Air Force Museum. This restored 109 has the Revi reflector gunsight at the top right of the instrument panel. The cannon breech cover is prominent between the rudder pedals. The yellow pipe to the left feeds the engine with fuel from the drop-tank. On the right, the yellow-striped black handle is the throttle.

C   At the pilot's left hand are two wheels. The outboard wheel is the emergency undercarriage-raising control; the inboard wheel trims the "flying tail."

D   The pilot's right-side panel. At the top are the circuit breakers for the fighter's electrical system, and below are the controls for supplying the oxygen essential for the high-altitude flying which was so much a part of Bf 109 operations.

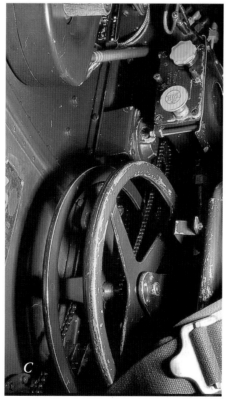

A

A   Before every flight, the pilot carries out a careful inspection of his fighter. Here he checks the freedom of movement of the leading edge slats.

B   Checking for full and free movement of all control surfaces is essential. The pilot is wearing a life preserver, required for all overwater flights. The pilot inflated the life preserver by activating a CO_2 cartridge at the bottom of the vest, or he could inflate it manually by blowing into the rubber tube attached to the vest just below his chin. The circular attachment to the tube is a survival compass.

C   The counterweight under the control surface helps to balance the aileron.

B

A   A close inspection of the undercarriage is vital. Wheels and brakes are looked at carefully, and the tires are examined for cuts, creep, and wear. The Bf 109 is very susceptible to accidents when in motion on the ground.   The pilot is wearing "Channel Trousers," with large pockets for necessary flight and survival equipment. Attached to his flight boot is a bandolier of color-coded flares.

B   The propeller is checked for any nicks, scratches, or imperfections. Serious flaws could lead to big problems when a propeller is spinning at high speed at the urging of a Daimler-Benz engine demanding maximum thrust.

C   The radio aerials need to be checked for breaks and kinks in the wire. The red control lock holds the rudder in place when the fighter is parked between missions. Removal of the lock is a very important part of the pilot's preflight checklist.

C

A   Before the pilot enters the fighter, he checks inside the cockpit. The step from the ground onto the wing is something of a stretch. The egg-shaped fairings just below the front windscreen are to attach a shade umbrella to the fighter, to keep the cockpit at least a few degrees cooler, in the North African sun. This Bf 109, "Black Six," was in service in Libya before capture.

B   The pilot swings his leg over the side of the cockpit, holds onto the windshield frame, and lowers himself into the very snug-fitting cockpit.

C   The canopy is hinged on the right side and is very heavy. The pilot reaches up and lowers it over his head, taking care not to have his other hand on the cockpit rail. Behind the pilot, a steel plate helps to protect him from rear attacks.

B

C

A

B

A   The engine of Bf 109 "Black Six" is run up prior to takeoff. Bringing any aircraft high-performance piston engine up to operating temperatures before flight is important to prolonging its life. However, sitting on the ground too long with the engine running can send the temperatures soaring to dangerous levels.

B   "Black Six" taxis to the runway.

C   With the Daimler-Benz engine at takeoff power, the fighter takes off from the grass. The British Ministry of Defence requires the pilots selected to fly "Black Six" always to use grass runways, unless an emergency dictates otherwise.

D   The Bf 109 makes a low pass. In 1942, this was an encouraging sight for the soldiers of the Wermacht fighting in North Africa, but one which made their opposite numbers distinctly nervous.

Following pages: The clean lines of Willy Messerschmitt's classic fighter are apparent. The small cockpit just nudges into the airflow. The yellow triangle over the black six marks the filler cap for the fuselage fuel tank.

C

D

"Black Six" over a village in Kent in southern England. The fairings for the twin 13 mm machine guns are visible ahead of the cockpit; the muzzle for the 20 mm cannon shows on the point of the white spinner.

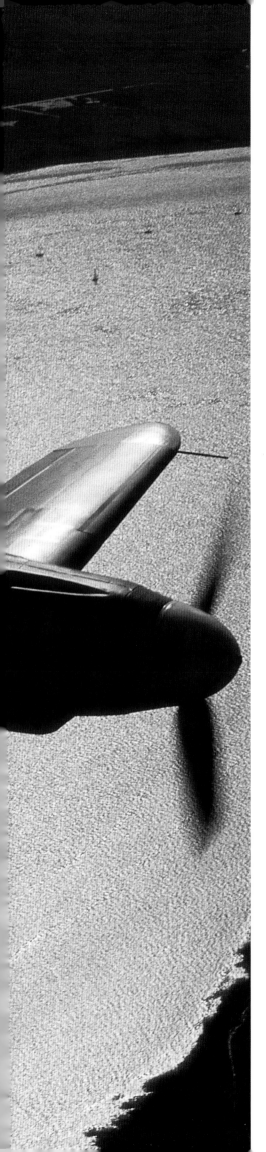

B

A   Backlit by a September sun, "Black Six" flies over a small estuary leading into the English Channel, a sight that would have been familiar to Luftwaffe pilots in WWII, particularly in 1940.

B   The Bf 109G-2 displays its desert camouflage, perhaps a little out of place against the fields of southern England.

Acknowledgments

The photographs done for this book would not have been possible without the considerable help of the following individuals and organizations.

Clive Denney, Historic Flying Limited. Clive's efforts and enthusiasm led me to the right people at Duxford's airfield and "Black Six." He also made it possible to shoot the air-to-air photographs of the Messerschmitt over the English Channel and countryside, while he flew a Mark IX Spitfire, to be seen in an upcoming book. Clive's wife, Linda, and their sons, Glenn and Andrew, fed me and made me feel at home.

Martin Sergeant, Goudhurst, Kent, UK. Martin flies an immaculate North American Harvard, G-BGOR, from his grass strip. His specialty, among many talents, is the restoration and maintenance of Bentley and Rolls-Royce automobiles. Martin and I experienced the unique thrill of flying in formation with two famous fighters over the Battle of Britain Memorial near Folkstone, on the weekend that commemorates the battle.

Flt. Lt. Charlie Brown, RAF Cranwell. This talented pilot, an RAF flight instructor, is one of the very few who are allowed to fly "Black Six."

Russ Snadden and the Messerschmitt Bf 109 "Black Six" team: Graham Snadden, Paul Blackah, Frank Aldridge, John Elcome, Chris McKay, Ian Mason, and Audrey Kinghorne. This dedicated group continues to give time and talent to keeping this unique combat veteran in the air. Whenever they stopped to brew up some tea, they included me in their circle.

Mark Hanna and his talented team of mechanics: Roger Shepherd, Chief Engineer; Martin Thompson; Tim Fane; and Ray Caller from The Old Flying Machine Company, Duxford. They maintain the Bf 109G-10 as a flying example of the late-war version of the fighter. Mark also let me use their office as a home base for operations while I was in the UK, and I appreciate the hospitality.

Victor Vick, whose unbelievably extensive collection and knowledge of Luftwaffe uniforms and flight equipment made the collage at the front of this book possible.

David Henchie, Airfield Manager at Duxford. Mr. Henchie made it possible to photograph "Black Six" in detail and during ground operations. He cut through a lot of red tape for me and made access to the airplane possible.

Don Lopez, Deputy Director, National Air and Space Museum. Mr. Lopez made it possible to photograph Günther Rall and Walter Schuck in the cockpit of the museum's restored Bf 109.

Lee Yenson, Corringham, Essex, UK. A living historian who became the Luftwaffe pilot in the photographs for this book.

My kids, Nate, Brigitta, and Joe. Also my parents, Bill and Jane Patterson, for helping me with the kids when I am chasing airplanes as well as for their ongoing support.

Ross and Elinor Howell, Howell Press. Ross continues to believe in and support what I do and how I do it.

Ron Dick, my compatriot, friend, and partner. We keep finding things to do books about.

Cheryl Terrill, for an understanding friendship.

I would also like to thank the following for helping to make this book possible: Kurt Wiedner, David Farnsworth, Jeffrey Ethell, David Hake, and Paul Perkins.

Technical Notes

The original photography in this book was all done with the intent to as faithfully as possible remove the clues of the present day and try to look back through a window opened by the owners and operators of these aircraft, a window into the 1940s when formations of these airplanes flew over the European continent during World War II.

I used a variety of cameras and equipment to complete this project: a Wista 4x5 Field View camera with a 150mm Caltar II lens and a 90mm Nikkor lens; a Mamiya RB67 with 50mm, 90mm, and 180mm lenses; a Nikon F3 with a motor drive and a Nikon 8008 with a garden variety of Nikkor lenses.

All the photographs were shot as transparencies to make the best possible color separations.

The 4x5 and 6x7 photos were all shot on Kodak Ektachrome Daylight film. The 35mm photos were taken with Ektachrome Lumiere.

The concept, design, and the photographs are done by Dan Patterson, 6825 Peters Pike, Dayton, Ohio 45414.

Bibliography

Brown, Eric. *Wings of the Luftwaffe*. New York: Doubleday, 1978.

Deighton, Len and Max Hastings. *Battle of Britain*. London: Michael Joseph, 1990.

Donald, David. *Wings of Fame, Vol. 4*. London: Aerospace Publishing, 1996.

Galland, Adolf. *The First and the Last*. London: Methuen, 1955.

Green, William. *Warplanes of the Third Reich*. New York: Galahad Books, 1970.

Green, William and Gordon Swanborough. *The Complete Book of Fighters*. New York: Smithmark, 1994.

Grinsell, Robert, Bill Sweetman, et al. *The Great Book of WW2 Airplanes*. New York: Bonanza Books, 1984.

Hardesty, Von. *Red Phoenix*. Washington, DC: Smithsonian Institution, 1982.

Herrmann, Hajo. *Eagle's Wings*. Shrewsbury, UK: Airlife Publishing, 1991.

Howson, Gerald. *Aircraft of the Spanish Civil War*. Washington, DC: Smithsonian Institution, 1990.

van Ishoven, Armand. *Messerschmitt Bf 109 at War*. New York: Charles Scribner's Sons, 1977.

Jablonski, Edward. *Air War*. New York: Doubleday, 1979.

Mason, Frank. *Battle over Britain*. London: McWhirter Twins, 1969.

Middlebrook, Martin. *The Schweinfurt-Regensburg Mission*. London: Allen Lane, 1983.

Mitcham, Samuel. *Eagles of the Third Reich*. Shrewsbury, UK: Airlife Publishing, 1989.

Murray, Williamson. *Strategy for Defeat*. Secaucus, NJ: Chartwell Books, 1986.

Musciano, Walter A. *Messerschmitt Aces*. Blue Ridge Summit, PA: TAB Books, 1989.

Nowarra, Heinz J. *Die 109*. Stuttgart, Germany: Motorbuch-Verlag, 1979.

Price, Alfred. *The Hardest Day*. London: MacDonald & Jane's, 1979.

_____. *The Last Year of the Luftwaffe*. Osceola, WI: Motorbooks, 1991.

Shores, Christopher. *Air Aces*. Greenwich, CT: Bison Books, 1983.

Taylor, John W.R. *Combat Aircraft of the World*. New York: G.P. Putnam's Sons, 1969.

Time-Life Editors. *The Luftwaffe*. Chicago: Time-Life Books, 1982.

Toliver, Raymond and Trevor Constable. *The Blond Knight of Germany*. Blue Ridge Summit, PA: TAB Books, 1970.

_____. *Fighter Aces of the Luftwaffe*. Fallbrook, CA: Aero Publishers, 1977.

Wood, Derek and Derek Dempster. *The Narrow Margin*. London: Tri-Service Press, 1990.

Wood, Tony and Bill Gunston. *Hitler's Luftwaffe*. London: Salamander Books, 1977.

Dan Patterson is a self-employed photographer, graphic designer, and private pilot living in Dayton, Ohio. Previous books are *Shoo Shoo Baby, A Lucky Lady of the Sky, The Lady: Boeing B-17 Flying Fortress, The Soldier: Consolidated B-24 Liberator, Mustang: North American P-51, Lancaster: RAF Heavy Bomber,* and *American Eagles: A 50th Anniversary Review of The United States Air Force and Its Origins.*

Ron Dick served for 38 years in the Royal Air Force, accumulating over 5,000 hours in more than 60 types of aircraft. He retired from the service as an Air Vice-Marshal in 1988 following a tour as the British Defence Attache in Washington, D.C. He now lives in Virginia, writing and lecturing generally on military and aviation history. Previous books are *Lancaster: RAF Heavy Bomber* and *American Eagles: A 50th Anniversary Review of the United States Air Force and Its Origins.*